Death at Quebec

Death at Quebec

And Other Poems

Don Gutteridge

This edition
published as Part One
of the 1971 edition previously published by
Fiddlehead Poetry Books

Wet Ink Books
www.WetInkBooks.com
WetInkBooks@gmail.com

Copyright © 2022 Wet Ink Books
Copyright © 2022 Don Gutteridge

All rights revert to the author. All rights for book, layout and design remain with Wet Ink Books. No part of this book may be reproduced except by a reviewer who may quote brief passages in a review. The use of any part of this publication reproduced, transmitted in any form or by any means, electronic, mechanical, photocopied, recorded or otherwise stored in a retrieval system without prior permission in writing from the publisher or a licence from The Canadian Copyright Licensing Agency (Access Copyright) is prohibited. For an Access Copyright licence, visit: www.accesscopyright.ca or call toll free: 1.800-893-5777.

Death at Quebec: And Other Poems
by Don Gutteridge

Cover Image – "A creepy cabin in the woods"
      by Solarseven / Shutterstock. Used by permission.
Cover Design – Richard M. Grove
Layout and Design – Richard M. Grove
Typeset in Garamond
Printed and bound in Canada
Distributed in USA by Ingram,
    – to set up an account – 1-800-937-0152

Library and Archives Canada Cataloguing in Publication

Title: Death at Quebec / Don Gutteridge.
Names: Gutteridge, Don, 1937- author.
Description: Poems. | Previously published: Fredericton, N.B.: Fiddlehead Poetry Books, 1971.
Identifiers: Canadiana 20220241686 |
    ISBN 9781989786703 (softcover)
Classification: LCC PS8513.U85 D4 2022 |
    DDC C811/.54—dc23

Table of Contents

Epilogue: A poem for four voices
    1 – The Jesuits in Huronia – *p. 2*
    2 – Champlain – *p. 5*
    3 – Hudson – *p. 8*
    4 – Riel – *p. 11*

– Death at Quebec – *p. 16*
– Brebeuf on the Cross – *p. 24*

– La Salle: Fragments from a Journal
    – Part Two – *p. 28*
    – Part Two – *p. 38*

Short Author Bio – *p. 49*

Epilogue

A poem for four voices

1 The Jesuits in Huronia

Bringing our Word
we came
to what we thought
was wilderness

Knew
the hard spring
rivers rock
against the cross
of muscle   bone
down the spine
we kept
as secret joy
(remembered Calvaries)

Knew
a wind of ice
flung like shale
against the flesh
(St. Stephen upright
leaning into pain)
and winter then
providing snow
and wilderness enough
for forty Moses

Bringing our Light
we came
to what we thought
was Darkness,
and found

These faces
bright with summer
innocence and
knowing of winter
running cold
in primal stone

Bringing our Gift
we came
to what we thought
was Emptiness,
and found

a rib of life
more green
than Adam's
dream of Eden
lost

And found

another name
for love
a masculinity
of pine and seed
of suns unrepressed
beneath the
mothering earth awaits
lightning's release:
electric darkness

Bringing our Light   our Gift
we came
bringing our Word
to what we thought was dumbness
of rock
of pagan rib

and found

a lightning shock
to numb the soul
dumbfounding flesh

Until we seemed
but only tongues
dropping syllables
into Chaos

and no reply
but
Babylon.

2 Champlain

When I left my name
in passing
on a river
on a lake
did it bleed
when spring came
to crack the ice
capillaries of
sudden freedom?
did it burn
with summer's
skin of sun and
water warm beneath?
did it die
with autumn and
slow funeral of leaves
moved thru river
before cold closed
on fall and all
there was of death?
till spring and
new transfusions
of sun
could make
another dying
for river
for lake
bearing my name.

But did the letters
bleed?
The syllables
burn?
My name admit to
death?

Or did it
(left in passing)
merely pass
the way
that all our names
must pass
when blood
is silent,
our bones mute?

And yet,
I *was* there:
on those rivers

that lake,
felt my
paddle-blade
touch a summer
running in the deep current
saw the
image of my death
in maples
exposed to sudden
wilderness of age,

measured the
quality of winter
ice corrosion
with a linkage
of my own.

Did I give
my name
(in passing)
to lake   to river?

Or did I give
my name up
to river and lake
in a passing
in a moving
beyond word
and name
to a last
syllable
of blood?

3 Hudson

When I came
to this place
to this wide bay
I had seen men die:
husk of their bodies
curved over
worm of scurvy
feeding inside,
had seen the
simple bullet
find a core
of flesh,
or blade break
a stem of
arm or leg,
letting death
in
and the eyes
reluctant
feeling it.

When I came
with my ship
and my self
to this place
I had seen
many deaths.

But there is no
death like this:
with the whole
sea soured
with fish rotting
in ice
of elemental graves,
and wind blowing
conflagration
of cold over
pine and tamarack
that have been
burned beyond
burning and
still green
somewhere
at the charred
brains of
their growing
at roots of rock
with grain of
resurrection
still in them.

There is no death
like this one:
my blood souring
and the sea around me,
my mind burning
with a wind's flame,
my flesh rotting
in an elemental grave,
and somewhere
with eyes just
beginning
I reach thru

charred remains of
flesh   bone   brain
for root of
resurrection
I never knew
till now
till this burning
till this death
on a wide bay
in the private ark
I built
of my self,
though ice
closes
elemental
over
me.

4 Riel

1

I am a man
as any man:

hands to know
the plough's hand
deeper in the earth,
hair to feel
the wind's
passing thru
and grasses move,
eyes to let
the sky's
vastness in
to deeper skies
I only know
because
my hands
my hair
these eyes
become a voice
to say

I am a man

2

There is no
eloquence to
blood running
from the mouths
of wounds and
battles lost,
the eyes of the dead
at Duck Lake
and Batoche are
white stones
darkening
at
the
centre

I hear
no story
of their suffering
no rhythm
of waters running
blue St. Lawrence
breathing tides
the earth-red
of my own river
blending to
seed of lakes
the world
may wait
a hundred suns
to see

When my body
swings like a
dead tongue
from the white-man's
scaffolding,
will there be
an eloquence
to tell…

or will this
prairie be
a coffin
for my voice
a dwelling place
for
two
white
stones?

5 The Last Word

Do our voices
reach out
from the past
escape the text
of history book
or turn
of politician's tongue,
describe a
true syllable
of what we knew
and still know
though words
are water
one can feel
and not define?

Or could there be
some secret part
of north
some centre
we never touched
in all our wandering,
some syllable
of silence
our tongues
did not dare
to desecrate,
some holy core

whose seed
we could not hope
to recognize as
altars running
fountains thru
the deep
earth-colour
of our blood.

Death at Quebec

The seigneur tells it

At first
the sun burned
our pink skin

warmth and
brandy-laughter in
the long house
Good Cheer, they said

our prayers
scented the
green chapel-wood

in there
I could smell
God

with *him*
our muskets make
the silence jump back
(it grows again
seamless   self-healing)
striding thru drifts to
the brown doe
dead against a
hump of snow
back-broken, like a stick
oh the blood-sweet
dark venison of her

our beards drip
with it
his mouth: a wound

Every year a child
grows out of her
like a tuber
a corn-blight sucking
nine months on the
stalk of her, but
ruptured spores breed:
the wind diseased –
the stem of her green once
once cradling my lust
I rooted in her
summered on her thighs
she caught the rain of
my sperm   O God the
ground gave way and we
both survived

Last night…again
she took it in her clay
crotch (like a carrot)
even my lust couldn't heal

her prayers
in the evening
are sweet breathing
are incense falling:
my ears speak

These sons of mine
(I saw them red-skinned
birth-blood still on them
pink worms
crawled out of that
clay seam   only her
screams gave my ear
pain, made it all
at least animal)
where will they find
an image of knowing?

I see them now
on rivers of noise
on the Ottawa
on the Richelieu
brains worn smooth
with endless paddling
their souls gone
to the beaver
(or some darker furring
among the bronzed
grease-glistening whores
spread-eagled on every
hump of granite)

And my fat daughters…
leeches that
feed on my love till
the bone gleams
pain   shines

This land will
not breed corn
but flies thrive
drink the cool
sun in

I have one son,
he tills the
brutal soil
fumbles prayers on
his thick tongue
obeys me with his body,
tills the ground lustily:
but there is no marriage
of sun and earth here,
he cannot beat the fields
into submission
his rage withers the corn

clay is stubborn
loves pain

"Pray to God," his mother said,

But he too has looked for Him
behind the shadow
under the ice
in the blind sun

There he is now!
He's broken the share
snapped it cross-grain
fingers too calloused
to feel the seam,
his tongue moves easy
in a furrow of curses

I will tell him!

But these dreams:

red-skinned squaw
on the domed snow
weakening where
thighs cross
articulate
O God   the gun
slides
blood-wet
into the sweet
dark deer-meat
of her...

Are these woods a
shadow around me or
in me?
the sun is thin with
shining thru them

This granite is older
than our first bone
is seamed with myth
with hieroglyphic runings
sealed by a silence
that stilled the
first and vital Word
(conspiracy of
sun   earth
and condoning sea)

This earth
made its covenant
with universal darkness
long before the God of
Abraham broke Chaos
with his lance
of light

Year by year
I sit
in the sun's thinning
my age growing around
me, the shadow
lengthens, grows
no darker, no
more light is let
thru the trees,
the dreams persist
but do not be-
come a dream,
will not give me
life nor death,
I watch my son
abuse the earth

he sprang from,
see his mother
stiffen because the
yearly child
no longer oils her
seam with blood,
think of my sons
dying graveless
the wind praying
over their bones –
somewhere a savage whore
tuberous bellied
full of black
spore the earth
will spit back at her
will spit back at me

because I sit
year by year
watch the seasons
rot and revive

The sun is
keen today
against the leather
of my skin,
is clean

and casts
no shadow

out or in

Brebeuf on the Cross

This pain
scrapes me
clean
(bone-knife skimming
pulpy flesh
from the hide:
oiled gleam is
holy in the sun)
makes life single
and singular:
blood   guts   bone
fuse on its point
merge with its
purpose   the
purple altars are
running with pus the
steeples burn
thru bloody cloud

This pain is
bearable and believable
delicious as
Eve's first and
only apple
my teeth squeeze
the white flesh
surrenders the
bitter and teeming
tumescent heart
at the core

my arms
break like
rotten crosses

My Christ!

do You hear them?

* * *

Was my Saviour's death
so absurd as this?

I dangle from
this crooked stake
like a scarecrow
without the authority
of even clothes –
the crows drop
their dung on me
with divine disdain,
savage laughter
rings with the
terrible innocence
of the child seeing,
I want to
giggle at my
own nakedness:
withered testes
strung like unpicked

grapes on a vine the
sun never loved,
not even the wind
could frighten my penis
into standing

My crow children
come unto me
with gifts of pain
that are
invisible strings:
I dance to
their mad puppetry

At last
my mouth gathers
all of its godly rage,
I utter one cry
just as the vine
discovers its
lost tumescence

even the jack-
pines blush.

Is God peeking?
does He feel
these strings
jerk childishly
in the face of
my ludicrous agony?

* * *

When the flowering stops
will the roots
be fingers
grounded in firmament,
or are they
of this exquisite burning
this delicious blood-blossom
which consumes
me

I feel it
carolling in my
private darkness
harmonic
and
pandemonial

O God!
is this grand
death Yours or
my own?

La Salle:
Fragments from a Journal

Part One

In March of 1680, LaSalle along
with four Frenchmen and an Indian
hunter set out on a thousand mile
journey from Fort Crevecoeur on
the Illinois River to Fort Frontenac
on Lake Ontario.

Out there
it seems so peaceful:
hot sun and icy lake
blend
without complaint,
trees release their
hoarded light

out there
the bush gathers
darkness, death
is numerous and
without sound:
no word to mark the
end of things
and no one
listening…

but

beneath this conspiring serenity
what scenes of
pantomimic terror?
what acts of wordless fury?

* * *

They do not know
the wood has already
devoured them
beaks have picked out
eyes for berries,
claws tasted flesh,
cold nested in
the marrow-warmth

heat has brooded
too long in the
cellulose chambers,
lightning flooded the
cranial rooms:
cells are not
waterproof

They do not know
melon-seed is
spilled semen the
ground spits back

winged   burred wind and
water-blown seed
salts flesh,

uproots capillaries
broods an embryonic
dream of death

(pine-cone is a
wire worm in the
flaccid penis:
crows make it
their carrion home)

They do not know
wind sings insanity
to the listening brain
the sun is a
bright leech the
heart loves

and winter dines
on the warmth
a bone leaves

* * *

I've seen the
slick of my blood
on dead rock:
berry-juice for
lewd tongues,
wandering bear (or sun)
to lick

We don't feel truth
till our gut breaks
of it
and we die
with the stink
in our mouths

* * *

Tonight
I ordered them
not to light it

they think that I
and not the cold
am their enemy

But snow's pain
is impersonal:
I can feel
the shape of my
bones where the
flesh was,
they are
comfortable

After a while
we despise

fire

* * *

Cold, like pain,
is a companion
he puts the blade
in lovingly

leaves the
bone clean

* * *

They are drowsy,
want to sleep:

it is their death
wishing its way
into the brain

Cold gives me
the clarity of pain,
when I walk
I know an outline
of bone
angle and direction
beneath the
superfluous flesh
become believable

* * *

Sun and snow
have made light useless,
the brain pulls
its eyes inward
to warm and
illuminating darkness.

When it is time
I will let
my body sleep:
the mind knows
where it is going

* * *

What is blizzard
more than inner
curves moving,

a darkness
in reverse?

* * *

Tonti:
your iron claw
cuts two ways

inner wounding
like a foreign scar

you must continually
enclose with your
nativeness,

and

outward first
by which we all
know you,

Even I
must shake that
rigid claw, feel
the flesh that
closes it

* * *

Pain gives a
form, is a
kind of knowing,
a direction we can
only contain
or occasionally
oppose.

My will
is my wound
outer and inner:
granite and distance
the unloving total
quality of this land
is apocalyptic pain
my body
contains

* * *

Moving
is its own space
my pain fulfills

and love is
a kind of
moving

* * *

This wind is a
blizzard of blood
a harvest of nails

I
love them

* * *

This stretch of
rock and evergreen
these endlessly
stationary rivers
are distance
are time
are the real cross
Christ stretched his
body on

And his Agony
is our going together
thru a winter garden
with its stations of

ice and snow
(sun abandoned,
wind rehearsing doom
in the pines)
is our mutual blood
left against the
centuries of trees,
is repetition of our
scarred feet on
millennial granite,
is the shared energy of
our walking
which is become
a voyage
(not to water-
falling innocence,
a Great River's source,

not to the hewn
and blocked sanctuary
of European pride)
but a voyage
which is no longer
a voyage at all
but a
journeying

Part Two

In 1684, LaSalle, with four ships and two hundred colonists, attempted to land at the mouth of the Mississippi River. However, they missed their target, and landed in Texas. Several attempts were made to find the River, and on the last of these LaSalle was murdered by a group of conspirators from his own party...

This south-
ness winds into my flesh
rains in my blood
builds a private storm
each cell magnifies
each nerve articulates

the brain cannot
contain...

Ah, Christ,
where is your
northern and sheer
bone-directing
love?

* * *

Remembering that other journey…

river spurting and
strong like a
cut artery

they grumbled
more than usual

strange that I
never feel the
strain of muscle
the tortured palms,
except when we stop
and the pain comes
in great ejaculations!

Do I keep it
locked and sacred
in some inner space
to be spilled, later,
on the ground?

On the water
there is never pain,
at least, not mine.
Perhaps I share
the river's

Each tree brings
its own face:

I see their
angular pain,
their bevelled and
elongated pride,
the wind in
them is incessant
ancestral whispering:
I feel their
cranial longing:
tribal nerves quiver
in my glacial dark

sudden flood of
sun   ice
articulates at last
bones of the
dead centuries
move in these
faces move in
me

The river below us
flings its brown arms
over the shouldering granite:

here, all land
is island,
water encompasses and defines
the current that
carries us so
wilfully is
line and direction

I put my paddle
in and feel the
tilt of the sea.

How can I tell them
we can be lost –

do not know what
island of rock
will be brought
eventually to us –
and yet be
found because the
river is both
brine and blood
and ocean is
ultimately human?

* * *

They think we are
lost again…
and we are

but the river
has a mind
of its own

* * *

They are crazed with it,
dragging that
Indian doe
into the green bush
jamming their
European tubers into the
nest of her groin...

She sheds them
like disused leaves and
the bush welcomes
her greeness back:
a wound received.

They lie there now
in a semen daze:
limp dreams in their hands
do not tell
the implacable vengeance
of granite and wood.

Inside
my own seed
boils in
scrotal darkness
drives its pro-
genitive longings
back thru blood:
they sear my
brain like
hot stars like
cosmic
branding irons.

* * *

They are plotting again,
who will put the
first bullet in my brain,
who will give me
an insignificant end.

They do not know
the magnitude of
death.

* * *

Here, death is
palpable —

a slit throat
blood still bubbling
white bone
shining thru the
cruciform core

or the carcass
of a stag
gutted by wolves
(did he believe
his death even as
the Roman jaws
embraced his throat,
loved his blood?)
or that Senecan chief

and his family
found in the
northern spring with
snow's release:
gathered still
in a last
supper of pain

a kind of
communal dying
(did they,
having tasted enough of
hunger   winter,
at last
love death?)
eyes still open:
to let
the universe
in?

* * *

One is lost
not when the place
is strange,
only when direction
fails

* * *

They are whispering again:
I am arrogant, they say,
they plot against me,
hope to humiliate me
with the King.

They cannot know
my humiliation:

I am naked
on the stake
of the universe,
shiver in
polar winds,
continental elements
conspire against me
the sun is sprung loose
from God's orbit,
the land and I
are Armageddon
without end,
together we tear off
lids from the Seven Seals,
apocalyptic horses
thunder inside us

we hurl our
separate cries back thru
Chaos and the
dying Light
to the first
presumptuous atom

a cry that is
our arrogance
our selves loosed
from tides-pull
from the systolic screams
of sun and blood

surely this is
Christ's cry flung out
at the centuries
from a pair of
crossed sticks stuck
in a mound of dust

while the cosmic
thunder laughs

surely this
is the ultimate
arrogance

* * *

My death is
south
insinuating
sheer bone

and moss
on the north side
of my brain.

Don Gutteridge was born in Sarnia and raised in the nearby village of Point Edward. He taught High School English for seven years, later becoming a Professor in the Faculty of Education at Western University, where he is now Professor Emeritus. He is the author of more than seventy books: poetry, fiction and scholarly works in pedagogical theory and practice. He has published twenty-two novels, including the twelve-volume Marc Edwards mystery series, and forty books of poetry, one of which, Coppermine, was short-listed for the 1973 Governor-General's Award. In 1970 he won the UWO President's Medal for the best periodical poem of that year, "Death at Quebec." Don lives in London, Ontario.

Email: gutteridgedonald@gmail.com.